THE PLIGHT OF American health care is best told through the eyes of a seventh-grader named Deamonte Driver.

Deamonte was born on the wrong side of the tracks, in Prince George's County, Md. Prince George's was founded in 1696 and was named for the Danish prince who married Queen Anne of Great Britain. In 1791, a chunk of the county was ceded to help create the District of Columbia.

Today, Prince George's sits directly east of the nation's capital. Aided by the decades-long expansion of federal spending, Prince George's is now the wealthiest county in America in which the majority of the population is black. But Deamonte was not one of the wealthy ones. He was an African-American child on welfare. He was raised by a single mother. He spent his childhood in and out of homeless shelters. He died in 2007, at the age of 12.

Deamonte, however, did not die in a drive-by shooting, or in a drug deal gone bad. He died of a toothache.

In September 2006, Deamonte started

complaining to his mother, Alyce, that his teeth hurt. Alyce started calling around, looking for a dentist who would see him. But every dentist she called said no. Months later, after she had made several dozen phone calls, she found one.

The dentist she finally found told her that her son had six abscessed teeth, and he recommended that Deamonte see a surgeon to take them out. That took another round of phone calls. It took another several months for Alyce to find Deamonte an oral surgeon who was willing to take the job.

Within a week of the long-anticipated surgical appointment, Deamonte told his mother that his head ached. It turned out that the infection from one of his abscessed teeth had spread to his brain. Deamonte was taken to the hospital, where he underwent emergency brain surgery. He got better for a while but began to have seizures and was operated on again. Several weeks later, Deamonte was dead.

According to Ezra Klein of the *Washington Post*, Deamonte Driver's story shows us why

> *There are many problems with Obamacare. But the law's cruelest feature is what it will do to low-income Americans who are already struggling.*

it would be immoral to repeal the Affordable Care Act, a.k.a. Obamacare, a law that strives to expand health insurance coverage to the uninsured. "To repeal the bill without another solution for the Deamonte Drivers of the world? And to do it while barely mentioning them? We're a better country than that. Or so I like to think."

But Deamonte Driver did not die because he was uninsured. Indeed, Deamonte Driver died because he *was* insured – by the government. It turns out that Deamonte was on Medicaid.

* * *

Obamacare does not offer better health care to the Deamonte Drivers of the world. Under Obamacare, if Deamonte were still alive today, he would still be stuck with the same dysfunctional Medicaid coverage that he was stuck with before. Indeed, Medicaid is likely to get much worse. According to the Congressional Budget Office, Obamacare will shove 17 million *more* Americans into Medicaid, the developed world's worst health care system.

There are many problems with Obamacare. But the law's cruelest feature is what it will do to low-income Americans who are already struggling. Study after study shows that patients on Medicaid do no better, and often do worse, than those with no insurance at all.

There is a way to provide high-quality health care to the poor, one that would spend substantially less than Medicaid while ensuring that low-income Americans are protected against costly medical bills. But to understand the solution, we must first understand what went wrong.

* * *

It may seem strange to say this, but Medicaid – a program that in 2013 cost taxpayers more than $450 billion – started out as an afterthought. In the 1930s, '40s, and '50s, American progressives believed that the most politically palatable way to expand government sponsorship of health care was to begin with the elderly.

After all, the elderly were a far more sympathetic group in the public's eyes. Older Americans had less opportunity to earn their own money in order to fund their health care and were therefore generally poorer than other Americans, along with being less healthy. Being both relatively poor and relatively unhealthy, they were, in turn, also less likely to have health insurance. And policymakers believed that the model of Social Security as a "self-financed" program for the elderly, paid for with a dedicated payroll tax, could easily be extended to health insurance.

For many years, however, these efforts to expand government-sponsored health insurance were successfully opposed by a coalition in Congress of Republicans and conservative Democrats. They were also opposed by the organized force of American doctors, who feared that socialized medicine would restrict their freedom to serve their patients as they thought best.

In 1961, the American Medical Association (AMA) organized an early attempt by progressives to erect a universal, single-payer health-insurance program for the elderly. "Operation Coffee Cup," as the AMA called it, involved asking doctors' wives to organize coffee klatches in order to persuade their friends to write letters to Congress opposing the single-payer bill. At the meetings, the wives would play a recording narrated by an actor named Ronald Reagan, who warned that the single-payer bill "was simply an excuse to bring about what [progressives] wanted all the time: socialized medicine." The bill was defeated.

This dynamic, in which the AMA and congressional conservatives blocked government-sponsored health care, shifted dramatically in 1964, when Barry Goldwater challenged Lyndon Johnson for the presidency.

It would have been tough for any Republican to beat LBJ that year. Johnson, John F. Kennedy's vice president, had gained a substantial measure of sympathy after Kennedy was assassinated in November 1963. "In your heart, you know he's right," said a campaign ad for Goldwater the following year. But after Goldwater proclaimed that "extremism in the defense of liberty is no vice," Johnson's campaign retorted, "In your guts, you know he's nuts."

Democrats gained 36 seats in the House of Representatives – giving them an astonishing 155-seat majority – and increased their already huge Senate majority by two seats, nudging them up to a 36-seat majority. (By comparison, the substantial majorities Democrats held after the 2008 election were merely 79 seats in the House and 20 seats in the Senate.) Even taking conservative-leaning Democrats into account, liberals were utterly in control of Washington in 1965.

Suddenly, Democrats found themselves with a mandate to enact far-reaching reforms, and they did not waste the opportunity. Wilbur Mills, a conservative Democrat who chaired the key House Ways and Means Committee, had been a reliable obstacle to

---

The states with the worst Medicaid reimbursement rates also had the lowest rates of physician acceptance of new Medicaid patients.

---

progressive legislation. After the 1964 election, he decided to shepherd LBJ's bill through Congress.

The first bill of the 1965 congressional session – H.R. 1 in the House and S. 1 in the Senate – was titled "Hospital Insurance for the Aged Through Social Security." The focus on hospital insurance reflected the fact that hospitalization costs represented the greatest financial burden on the elderly at the time.

As the "Medi-care" Bill zipped through Congress, Republican leaders, still reeling and disoriented from their painful defeat, criticized the proposal from the left, arguing that the legislation was inadequate because it covered neither physician services nor prescription drugs and because it offered equal subsidies to seniors regardless of income. Mills called their hand and raised them, creating a new program for physician services called Medicare Part B – and a separate health care entitlement for the poor, regardless of age, called Medicaid.

President Johnson signed the Medicare and Medicaid provisions into law, amending the Social Security Act on July 30, 1965. Johnson gave former President Harry Truman the first Medicare card. The AMA and its physician members eventually reconciled themselves to Medicare. The program, in its early decades, let doctors charge whatever they wanted, creating a kind of unlimited slush fund for physicians that was funded by taxpayers. Costs skyrocketed.

Medicaid, on the other hand, was to be jointly funded by state governments along with Washington. State governments, with their balanced-budget amendments, borrowing restrictions, and limited funds, did not have the latitude to absorb runaway costs.

"Though adopted together, Medicare and Medicaid reflected sharply different traditions," wrote Paul Starr in *The Social Transformation of American Medicine.* "Medicare was buoyed by popular approval and acknowledged dignity of Social Security; Medicaid was burdened by the stigma of public assistance. While Medicare had uniform national standards for eligibility and benefits, Medicaid left the states to decide how extensive their programs would be. Medicare allowed physicians to charge above what the program would pay; Medicaid did not and participation among physicians was far more limited.

The objective of Medicaid was to allow the poor to buy into the 'mainstream' of medicine, but neither the federal government nor the states were willing to spend the money that would have been required."

* * *

The fact that Medicaid is jointly funded by the states and the federal government has had a consequential role in its evolution. The share that states pay, relative to Washington, is determined by a formula called the Federal Medical Assistance Percentage (FMAP). Title XIX of the Social Security Act, which now contains the Medicaid program, specifies that the federal government will contribute no less than 50 percent of a state's Medicaid costs.

The actual percentage of Medicaid spending that the federal government will sponsor varies depending on the relative wealth of a given state. In the nation's poorest state, Mississippi, Washington provides 73 percent of the funds; in wealthier states, like Massachusetts and New York, Washington pays the minimum 50 percent. Today, the median state enjoys an FMAP of 60 percent.

That means that for every dollar a state spends on its Medicaid program, the federal government will kick in an additional $1.50. It's not every day that a state politician gets to spend one dollar of his constituents' money and gain credit for spending nearly $2.50 in return. But that's how Medicaid works. As a result, irresponsible officials in many states have ratcheted up their Medicaid spending, knowing that taxpayers in other states will be forced to foot a good chunk of the bill.

Even then, the money eventually runs out. But by that point, hundreds of thousands of poor state residents have enrolled in the program, and governments are loath to throw them off the rolls. The federal Medicaid statute specifically bars states from charging higher premiums or co-pays to Medicaid enrollees, which would normally be a very effective way to save money.

As a result, states have one option that

they use more than any other to keep their Medicaid costs in check: they pay hospitals and doctors less to provide the same amount of care to the same number of patients.

"As in previous years, provider rate restrictions were the most commonly reported cost containment strategy," concludes an extensive 2012 review of state-based changes to Medicaid by the Kaiser Family Foundation. "A total of 39 states restricted provider rates in [fiscal year] 2011 and 46 states reported plans to do so in [fiscal year] 2012."

It has gotten so bad that in the average state, for every dollar that a private insurer pays a primary-care physician to care for a patient, Medicaid pays 52 cents. Of the 10 Medicaid states, including Washington, D.C., that pay doctors the least, nine are reliably blue states with left-leaning politics and expansive Medicaid programs: New York (where Medicaid pays 29 percent of what private insurers do), Rhode Island (29 percent), New Jersey (32 percent), California (38 percent), D.C. (38 percent), Maine (42 percent),

Florida (44 percent), Illinois (46 percent), Minnesota (46 percent), and Michigan (47 percent).

Now imagine you're a primary-care doctor with a busy practice. Two people call asking for an appointment to see you today, and you have one slot open. Do you give that slot to the patient who has private insurance, or the one who has Medicaid?

* * *

Actually, we don't even have to imagine. Sandra Decker, an economist for the National Center for Health Statistics at the Centers for Disease Control, did the work of correlating Medicaid's low rates to the percentage of doctors who accept new Medicaid patients, on a state-by-state basis. She found that primary-care doctors were 73 percent more likely to reject Medicaid patients relative to those who are privately insured, and specialists were 63 percent more likely to reject Medicaid patients.

Unsurprisingly, the states with the worst Medicaid reimbursement rates also had the lowest rates of physician acceptance of new Medicaid patients. Worst of all was New Jersey, where 60 percent of physicians were unwilling to accept new Medicaid patients. Next was California (43 percent), then Florida (41 percent), Connecticut (39 percent), Tennessee (39 percent), and New York (38 percent).

The fact that physicians reject Medicaid patients has real, human costs. In 2011, doctors at the University of Pennsylvania conducted a study, in which researchers posed as the parents of kids on Medicaid with urgent medical problems like acute asthma attacks or a broken forearm. They would call doctors in the relevant specialty and ask for appointments. If the "parents" told the doctors that their kids were on Medicaid, they were denied an appointment 66 percent of the time, compared with only 11 percent if they said they had private insurance.

In addition, the authors reported in the *New England Journal of Medicine*, at those clinics that accepted both Medicaid/SCHIP and privately insured children, the average wait time for an appointment was, on average, 22 days longer for those on Medicaid/SCHIP: 42 days vs. 20.

The health scenarios used in the study were all for kids with significant medical problems: persistent, uncontrolled asthma; acute depression; forearm fracture; new-onset seizures; type I diabetes; obstructive sleep apnea (difficulty breathing) and chronic ear infections; and severe atopic dermatitis (itchy rashes) that won't respond to conventional steroids. So, to put this in human terms: a

---

Despite the fact that we will soon spend more than $500 billion a year on Medicaid, Medicaid beneficiaries, on average, fared slightly worse than those with no insurance at all.

---

mother whose child has persistent, uncontrolled asthma has zero or a near-zero chance of being rejected by a doctor if the child has private insurance. However, if the child is on Medicaid or its sibling, SCHIP, the child has a 55 percent chance of not being able to get an appointment.

"It's very disturbing," said Dr. Karin Rhodes, one of the authors of the study, to Denise Grady of the *New York Times*. "As a mother, if I had a kid who was having seizures or newly diagnosed juvenile diabetes, I would want to get them in right away."

It's disturbing, all right, but hardly shocking to people who've experienced Medicaid's dysfunction firsthand. "It's interesting to think you even need a study to prove that," said Dr. Stephen Stabile of the Cook County Hospital system in Chicago. "It's pretty much common knowledge."

This isn't just a problem for kids with significant medical problems but also for those who need routine care. The June issue of the journal *Pediatrics* contains another study from the *New England Journal* authors, using the same methodology, in which they surveyed the ability of mothers to obtain urgent dentist appointments for their kids. In that study, 64 percent of Medicaid/SCHIP beneficiaries were unable to get an appointment, compared with a 5 percent rejection rate for those with private insurance: a ratio of 14 to 1.

* * *

There's a massive fallacy at the heart of Medicaid, and therefore at the heart of Obamacare. It's the idea that health insurance equals health care.

It doesn't take a PhD in health economics to appreciate that if you have a card that says you have health insurance, but that card doesn't get you into the doctor's office when you need help, you're not going to get better health care. But in case you were wondering, PhDs – and MDs – have looked at this problem. In 2010, a group of surgeons at the University of Virginia asked this question: Does the type of health insurance you have make a difference in the outcomes of the care you receive?

To answer it, they evaluated 893,658 major surgical operations from 2003 to 2007. The results were jarring. Patients on Medicare who were undergoing surgery were 45 percent more likely to die before leaving the hospital than those with private insurance; the uninsured were 74 percent more likely; and Medicaid patients were 93 percent more likely. That is to say, despite the fact that we will soon spend more than $500 billion a year on Medicaid, Medicaid beneficiaries, on average, fared slightly worse than those with *no insurance at all.*

The most obvious rebuttal to the Virginia surgeons' findings is, "Well, of course Medicaid patients did worse. People on Medicaid are poor, and poor people tend to be in poorer health than wealthy people." But the UVa authors anticipated this criticism. They normalized their figures to take relevant factors into account: age, gender, income, geographic region, operation, and health status.

The UVa study wasn't the first to show that Medicaid patients fare poorly. Other studies had found similar results:

A University of Pennsylvania study published in *Cancer* found that in patients undergoing surgery for colon cancer, the mortality rate was 2.8 percent for Medicaid patients, 2.2 percent for uninsured patients, and 0.9 percent for those with private insurance. The rate of surgical complications was highest for Medicaid, at 26.7 percent, compared with 24.5 percent for the uninsured and 21.2 percent for the privately insured.

A Columbia-Cornell study in the *Journal of Vascular Surgery* examined outcomes for vascular disease. Patients with clogged blood vessels in their legs or clogged carotid arteries (the arteries of the neck that feed the brain) fared worse on Medicaid than did the uninsured; Medicaid patients outperformed the uninsured if they had abdominal aortic aneurysms.

A study of Florida patients published in the *Journal of the National Cancer Institute* found that Medicaid patients were 6 percent more likely to have late-stage prostate cancer at diagnosis (instead of earlier-stage, a more treatable disease) than the uninsured; 31 percent more likely to have late-stage breast cancer; and 81 percent more likely to have late-stage melanoma. Medicaid patients did outperform the uninsured on late-stage colon cancer. (They were 11 percent less likely to have late-stage cancer).

A University of Pittsburgh study of patients with throat cancer, published in *Cancer*, found that patients on Medicaid or without insurance were three times as likely to have advanced-stage throat cancer at the time of diagnosis, compared with those with private insurance. Those with Medicaid or without insurance lived for a significantly shorter period than those with private insurance.

A Johns Hopkins study of patients undergoing lung transplantation, published in the *Journal of Heart and Lung Transplantation*, found that Medicaid patients were 8.1 percent less likely to be alive 10 years after their transplant operation, compared with those with private insurance and those without insurance. Medicaid was a statistically significant predictor of death three years after transplantation, even after controlling for other clinical factors. Overall, Medicaid patients faced a 29 percent greater risk of death.

You'd think that Medicaid's poor health outcomes would be a scandal on the left. You'd be wrong. After all, Obamacare puts 17 million more Americans into the Medicaid program. The law's supporters were placed in a bind: if Medicaid really does provide poor health outcomes, then they would have to admit that Obamacare is not all it was cracked up to be.

When Connecticut Senator Joe Lieberman said, in 2009, that he wouldn't support Obamacare if it expanded Medicare, the *Washington Post*'s Ezra Klein wrote, "Lieberman... seems willing to cause the deaths of hundreds of thousands of people in order to settle an old electoral score." Government-sponsored health care, Klein asserted, would save hundreds of thousands of lives. Opposing such a program was the moral equivalent of sanctioning mass murder.

The argument that Medicaid was not making poor people healthier seemed so counterintuitive – especially to those who believe in the efficacy of government programs – that most progressives dismissed it entirely.

Others portrayed a discussion of Medicaid's poor outcomes as a conspiracy designed to *harm* the poor. "The right wing's attack on government insurance programs has taken a novel and brash twist," wrote Jonathan Cohn in a *New Republic* article titled "The Conservative Assault on Medicaid." "If you're a thirty-something mother making, say, less than $20,000 as a hotel housekeeper, some conservatives think you'd be better off uninsured – i.e., completely at the mercy of charity care, depending in many cases on emergency rooms even for routine treatment – than if you had the government's insurance policy for the poor."

Fortunately, a group of leading health

economists – mainly based out of MIT and Harvard – took seriously the concerns about Medicaid's health outcomes and decided to design the definitive study that would prove that Medicaid made people healthier. The outcome of that study, published in 2013, would change the Medicaid debate forever.

* * *

The early 1990s were a heyday for progressive health reformers. Bill and Hillary Clinton famously campaigned for national health reform in 1992 and 1993; while that effort failed, a number of states led by Democratic politicians did their part to experiment with health-policy changes at the state level.

One of those states was Oregon. An emergency-room physician named John Kitzhaber, who also served in the Oregon State Senate, conceived of a plan to expand health coverage for the working poor, using the Medicaid program.

In 1993, before Kitzhaber's plan was approved by President Clinton, 240,000 Oregonians were on Medicaid. The following year, 120,000 additional residents enrolled. Spending on the program nearly doubled, from $1.33 billion in 1993-95 to $2.36 billion in 1999-2001.

The state budget buckled under the program's exploding costs. Something had to be done. So in 2003, the state passed a law clos-

---

Fire insurance doesn't prevent fires, and it isn't meant to. The purpose of fire insurance is to protect the policyholder from the catastrophic financial loss that occurs when one's home burns down.

---

ing the Medicaid program to new enrollees. That way, the rolls could gradually shrink over time, through attrition. In 2008, Oregon reopened the program to newcomers but limited the number of new spots to 30,000. Since nearly 90,000 Oregonians were on a Medicaid waiting list at the time, the state decided to hold a lottery to award the new Medicaid spots.

A group of economists from MIT and Harvard – including Kate Baicker, Amy Finkelstein, and Jonathan Gruber – realized that the problems in Oregon created an opportunity. For all the strengths of the Virginia study of surgical patients on Medicaid, that study had one all-too-common flaw: it was a *post hoc*, retrospective analysis of old patient records.

While such retrospective analyses can be useful, they run the risk of being infected with bias – the bias that hindsight is 20/20. The gold standard of experimentation, as with clinical drug trials, is a prospective, randomized experiment in which you study two populations, one with the desired treatment and one without, to see which fares better.

The Oregon lottery, the MIT and Harvard economists figured out, could allow the researchers to conduct just this kind of prospective, randomized experiment on Medicaid. The state had randomly offered Medicaid coverage to 30,000 residents, leaving tens of thousands more still uninsured. By tracking these patients over time, the economists could assess whether or not Medicaid was making its enrollees healthier. Were they living longer than uninsured Oregonians? Did they have fewer incidences of heart disease, diabetes, and the like?

In 2011, months after John Kitzhaber's inauguration as the 37th governor of Oregon, the economists released their initial findings. While it was too early to measure Medicaid's effects on objective health measures, such as blood pressure or cholesterol, patients told the researchers that they felt better about their health.

This rather modest result led to a chorus of jubilation from liberal journalists. "Amazing Fact! Science Proves Health Insurance Works," read a headline from Ezra Klein. Wrote Matthew Yglesias: "A new rigorous study from Oregon confirms that Medicaid does, indeed, save lives." (The study did not, in fact, detect any change in mortality.) Oregon's result "suggests that having health insurance substantially improves health," wrote David Leonhardt of the *New York Times*. One of the authors of the study, Amy Finkelstein of MIT, cheered, "What we found in a nutshell is that having Medicaid makes a big difference in people's lives."

There were problems with the first-year Oregon data. In their research paper, the investigators noted that two-thirds of the improvement in patients' self-reported health took place "about 1 month after [Medicaid] coverage was approved" but before the patients had seen a single doctor or consumed any health care services. This strongly suggested that the "benefit" that patients were reporting was the insurance version of a placebo effect. But this subtlety didn't make the front pages.

When the following July came around and it was time to publish the two-year results of the study, the Oregon investigators were strangely silent. The 2012 presidential election came and went. The state-by-state debate on expanding Medicaid, under Obamacare, came and largely went. Finally, on May 1, 2013 – 10 months late – the *New England Journal of Medicine* published the second-year findings. Did Medicaid save lives? No. It "generated no significant improvement in measured physical health outcomes," including death, diabetes, high cholesterol, and high blood pressure.

What's almost as striking as this nonresult is how few Oregonians felt the need to sign up for this allegedly lifesaving program. The authors report that of the 35,169 individuals who "won" the lottery to enroll in Medicaid, only 60 percent actually bothered to fill out the application. In the end, only half of those who applied ended up enrolling. Remember that this is a program on which we will be spending $7.4 trillion over the next 10 years, a program that Obamacare aims to throw 17 million more Americans into, because of the hundreds of thousands of lives that Medicaid will supposedly save.

Immediately, progressive bloggers went

into overdrive to explain these results away. "The sample size was too small," they said, even though new medicines for diabetes, high cholesterol, and high blood pressure routinely show significantly improved health outcomes in much smaller trials. "Two years isn't long enough to show a significant benefit," they insisted, even though new drugs that failed to show any benefit in two years would be summarily rejected by the FDA and abandoned by their sponsors.

The Medicaid cohort reported that they felt better about their health and their financial security as a result of enrolling in the program and were less depressed. We can presume that the 40 percent of Medicaid "winners" who didn't bother to fill out the application felt differently; they, however, were not surveyed.

Nonetheless, Medicaid's cheerleaders seized on this qualified bit of good news. "This is an astounding finding ... a huge improvement in mental health," said economist Gruber. To which conservative blogger

Ben Domenech responded, "I wonder whether we'd be better off replacing the [Medicaid] expansion with a program that hands out $500 in cold hard cash and a free puppy."

Austin Frakt of Boston University is a passionate Medicaid advocate who, for years, has disputed studies showing poor Medicaid outcomes. "That insurance ... improves health and reduces mortality risk is as close to an incontrovertible truth as one can find in social science," Frakt averred in 2010. Frakt had been holding up the Oregon study as the gold standard for health-policy research. Now that its results were out, he veered in both directions: he highlighted, as Gruber had, the alleged benefit in mental health, while simultaneously insisting that the Oregon study was "far too small" to draw meaningful conclusions.

Paul Krugman, the cantankerous columnist for the *New York Times*, dismissed the Medicaid skeptics this way: "If health insurance is a good idea – and you are nuts if you let this study persuade you otherwise – Medicaid is cheaper than private insurance. So where is

> *While Medicaid costs too much, its principal problem is that it doesn't make Medicaid patients healthier.*

the downside?" After that argument went nowhere, Krugman abruptly shifted gears, arguing that Medicaid's health outcomes don't matter. "Fire insurance is worthless!" he snarked. "After all, there's no evidence that it prevents fires."

Unwittingly, Krugman had stumbled onto the answer. There is a way to provide health coverage to the poor that truly protects them from medical calamities. But to do so, we must first learn from the way we insure ourselves against fires.

* * *

Paul Krugman is right. Fire insurance doesn't prevent fires, and it isn't meant to. The purpose of fire insurance is to protect the policyholder from the catastrophic financial loss that occurs when one's home burns down. In every sector of the economy except health care, that's what insurance is for. We buy car insurance, for example, to protect ourselves from the financial cost of car accidents. Yet when it comes to health care, we expect health insurance to save lives and improve health, instead of expecting it merely to protect us from catastrophic medical bills.

We could easily apply the lessons of car insurance and fire insurance to health insurance. But we don't, because many people have been persistently and ideologically opposed to treating health insurance this way. Imagine if car insurance also paid for your gasoline and your car washes. You'd use premium gas all the time and get the deluxe car wash once a week. But your insurance rates would go up too, because your extra consumption – and everyone else's – would drive up the cost of coverage.

This, indeed, is the bottom line from the Oregon study: that protecting people against bankruptcy from medical bills is a good thing and that auto- and fire-like catastrophic coverage is a far less costly way to do that, compared with expanding an already failed entitlement program.

We should make one thing clear: while Medicaid costs too much, its principal problem is that it doesn't make Medicaid patients healthier. It's not wrong to spend a large sum of money on health care for the poor. It is wrong to *waste* large sums of money on health care for the poor. There are so many market-based alternatives to Medicaid, alternatives that would offer uninsured, low-income Americans the opportunity to see the doctor of their choice and gain access to high-quality, private-sector health care.

Singapore, which has a universal system of catastrophic coverage and health-savings accounts, spends one-seventh of what we spend on health care, with comparable results. The HSA-catastrophic combination is meant to protect beneficiaries from large medical bills while giving them control over their own health spending. If we gradually replaced our $1.5 trillion-a-year health care behemoth with this approach, we could wipe out our budget deficit and permanently solve our entitlement crisis.

Indiana, under then-Governor Mitch Daniels, placed Medicaid patients on an inexpensive combination of high-deductible insurance and subsidized health-savings accounts. The program enjoyed a 98 percent approval rating among its participants. But the Obama administration has declined to renew Indiana's waiver to continue this program, insisting that it be replaced by traditional Medicaid.

But let's not tinker around the edges with Medicaid, like Indiana has had to. Let's build from scratch a new health program for low-income Americans, one that would actually offer better health care than many wealthy Americans receive.

* * *

It wouldn't be that hard. Start by paying a primary-care physician $80 a month to see each patient, whether he is healthy or sick. That's what so-called concierge doctors charge, and it would give Medicaid patients what they really need: first-class primary-care physicians to manage their chronic cardio-vascular and metabolic conditions.

Dr. Lee Gross is a co-founder of an innovative company called Epiphany Health. He offers "concierge plans for the little guy." Epiphany is designed primarily for individuals and families who don't have traditional health coverage. Unlike Deamonte Driver's mom, Alyce, who had to call dozens of doctors to find just one who would see her son, Epiphany's doctors are on retainer. You pay $83 a month and receive primary care whenever you need it. Spouses cost $69 extra, while kids cost $49.

"The most common medical conditions can be successfully managed at the primary care level, meaning most people do not need to see specialists," Gross writes on his website. "There is also no reason to end up in the emergency room for minor illnesses or injuries because you have no other option."

That's the dirty secret of Medicaid. You might have heard the rumor that uninsured people are clogging emergency rooms because the law allows them to get free care there. But the unreported story is that it is *Medicaid* patients who clog the emergency rooms because they can't persuade regular doctors to see them.

So give every Medicaid enrollee the Epiphany plan. Then throw on top of that a $2,500-a-year catastrophic plan to protect the poor against financial ruin. The total annual cost of such a program would be $3,460 per person, 42 percent less than what Obamacare's Medicaid expansion costs. Heck, you could put the entire country on that kind of plan, along with giving people the opportunity to use health savings accounts to cover the rest.

As a result of the 2012 Supreme Court decision that upheld the constitutionality of Obamacare, states have the freedom to choose whether or not to participate in the law's expansion of the Medicaid program. Though the expansion is largely funded from federal tax dollars, every state will still have to spend a considerable sum of its money to sign on to the Medicaid expansion.

Patrick Colbeck, an aerospace engineer turned Michigan state senator, proposed just this combination – retainer-based primary care and catastrophic coverage – as a substitute for Michigan's Medicaid expansion. "We can use this as an opportunity to ... not only accomplish the stated objectives of Obama-

---

Instead of making sure that America never sees another case like Deamonte Driver's, Obamacare moves people out of privately sponsored coverage and into Medicaid.

---

care but [also to] establish Michigan as a destination state for employers seeking quality affordable healthcare for their employees," said Colbeck in the summer of 2013.

But Michigan opted to pass the 1965-vintage Obamacare version of Medicaid instead.

It was an unfortunate decision. At a time when middle-income Americans are being squeezed by the health law's hikes to private health-insurance premiums, the expansion takes money from them in order to fund a broken program that doesn't improve health outcomes. Instead, we could offer the poor real primary care and real catastrophic coverage.

Many conservative opponents of the Affordable Care Act are concerned that the law costs too much, that it represents too much government intrusion into the lives of ordinary citizens. But the law's true weakness is that it endorses and expands the humanitarian scandal that is today's Medicaid program. Instead of making sure that America never sees another case like Deamonte Driver's, Obamacare moves people out of privately sponsored coverage and into Medicaid. It's a senseless and cruel policy.

The good news is that all over America, innovative doctors and policy entrepreneurs like Lee Gross and Patrick Colbeck are coming up with ways to bring health care for the poor — and the middle class — into the 21st century, into the age of e-mails and iPhones and text messages. What these trailblazers need is the support of millions of Americans who can help turn their ideas into law. Americans like you.

First American edition published in 2013 by Encounter Books, an activity of Encounter for Culture and Education, Inc., a nonprofit, tax exempt corporation. Encounter Books website address: www.encounterbooks.com

Manufactured in the United States and printed on acid-free paper. The paper used in this publication meets the minimum requirements of ANSI/NISO Z39.48–1992 (R 1997) (*Permanence of Paper*).

FIRST AMERICAN EDITION

LIBRARY OF CONGRESS
CATALOGING-IN-PUBLICATION DATA IS AVAILABLE

ISBN10: 1-59403-752-3
ISBN13: 978-1-59403-752-8
E-BOOK: 978-1-59403-753-5

10 9 8 7 6 5 4 3 2 1

SERIES DESIGN BY CARL W. SCARBROUGH